The Organic Dog Treat Cookbook

25 All-Natural Howling Good Recipes

The Happybothams

ISBN:1974098427
ISBN-13:9781974098422

DEDICATION

This is dedicated to my dear old dog Tex. He was one of the coolest dogs of all time, even though he liked to bring me dead animals as gifts

CONTENTS

CONTENTS

INTRODUCTION

The Happybotham Dog Treat Company was founded out of a desire to give our neighbors dogs tummies a break and provide healthier treats. Tired of looking at long lists of preservatives in all foods and low quality ingredients in dog treats, we at the Happybotham Dog Treat Company became inspired to create treats from quality ingredients from foods we know more about. We felt that all dogs deserve more. Honestly, a beef treat should actually contain beef, not a long list of chemicals and unpronounceable ingredients, right?

We also thought that everyone would love to have their own recipes they could whip up at home for their dogs on any day. Dogs can distinguish between these home-produced treats, we're convinced of it. So try them out! There are tons of recipes in this paperback to choose from, and we assure you your dog will be happy you gave it the effort.

WHY ORGANIC?

With people spending more time these days to find out where their food is produced and how it is made, it's not surprising that their focus should turn to wanting to know more about what they are feeding their pets. Some pet owners may also turn to this book out of exasperation because their pups are having difficulty with store-bought treats, with their sensitive stomachs erupting with every purchase of a new combination.

There are so many organic products out there to choose from you should have no problem finding the perfect ingredients to make your dog's treats from. And if you do have trouble finding an organic ingredient in any of the recipes, you can always exchange it for its non-organic equivalent.

SUBSITITUES

Baking dog biscuits is not rocket science. Things can be easily exchanged, added or omitted, depending on what you have available or what your dog likes. These recipes are all very easily adjustable. If you are making substitutions, just keep an eye on the dough consistency when mixing. If it's too dry, add more water. Too wet, add more flour. It's pretty simple. And keep an eye on the baking time. If they are browning faster than the time says, remove them from the oven. If they still look too light, add a few more minutes and keep an eye on them. Your dogs will love most things you make for them, so know they'll be happy even if you think you over or under-cooked them a bit. Just be sure the meats you add are prepared according to the directions in the recipes.

TOOLS OF THE TRADE

The following is a list of utensils and kitchen tools used in many of the recipes in the book: we highly recommend them. If you don't have them, there are alternatives to use, or you can mix and stir by hand. But from experience, we can say that the easier these are to make, the better. The more effort and mess that goes into these treats, the less likely you are going to want to make them again.

ROLLING PIN

So many of these recipes require you to roll out the dough before cutting it. You can use many different tools to cut the dough, but you really need a pin to roll it out. Use a large plastic food storage bag and place it between the floured dough and the pin- then roll away.

FOOD PROCESSOR

This is an amazing time saver! You can puree, chop and make peanut butter. It can also mix the dough for you, it cuts down on a lot of the work.

PARCHMENT PAPER

Makes clean up so easy! Line normal baking pans with parchment paper prior to baking the treats.

CUTTING MAT

Thin, plastic and dishwasher safe are the best! Great for their flexibility to be able to move your ingredients around easily.

LATEX GLOVES

These can save your hands from the smell of salmon, tuna or livers.

COOKING PANS

Most recipes call for a standard cookie sheet or jelly roll pan. Some recipes call for a muffin pan, mini muffin pan, mini loaf pans and square pans. Skip these recipes if you don't have the pans.

STORAGE TIPS

All recipes are homemade and free of preservatives. Store these in a plastic bag or container in the refrigerator. They will still mold, so store an amount you think you will use in one week.

If you make more than a week's worth, they can be frozen and thawed later or shared.

SOFT OR CRUNCHY TREATS

You know your dogs and their tastes or dietary needs. If you want the treats to be softer, cook them for less time or on a lower heat (definitely keep them in the refrigerator, too). If you want your treats to be crispier, cook them a longer time at a lower heat. Or, when they are finished cooking turn the oven off but leave them in there on the tray to cook for a few hours or overnight.

BAR-B-Q BETTY

1 cup organic oat flour

1 cup organic brown rice flour

1 cup ground organic chicken or beef (cooked)

1/2 cup oat bran

2 tablespoons BBQ sauce (no onions or sugar)

1 egg

1/2 cup water

Preheat oven to 375 degrees.

Combine all ingredients and mix until a dough forms. Roll out on a lightly rice floured surface to 1/4 " thickness. Use a cookie cutter to cut into shapes. Grease or line a cookie sheet with parchment paper, and place the cookies on the pan.

Bake 22-27 minutes. Allow to cool completely and store the treats in an airtight container in the refrigerator.

BUTTER MY BISCUIT

1 cup organic oat flour

1 cup organic brown rice flour

2 teaspoons organic baking powder

1/4 cup extra virgin olive oil or coconut oil

2 ground sweet Italian turkey sausages

1/3 cup chicken broth

Preheat oven to 450 degrees.

Place the sausages in a pot of water. Bring to a boil and allow to cook for 20 minutes. Careful, they will be hot! Remove from heat and run under cold water until cool enough to handle. Remove the sausage casings and finely grind the sausage in a food processor.

Combine the sausage with all other ingredients and mix until a dough forms. Roll the dough out on a lightly rice floured surface to 1/4 inch thick. Use a cookie cutter to cut into any shapes you would prefer. Place on a lined cookie sheet (with parchment paper).

Bake 22-27 minutes or until tops are golden brown. Remove from pan and allow to cool. Store in an airtight container in the refrigerator.

APPLE CINNA-MINIS

6 cups water

6 cups organic barley flour or almond flour

2 tablespoons organic cinnamon

8 ounces organic apple puree or apple sauce

Preheat the oven to 325 degrees.

Combine the ingredients in a bowl and mix thoroughly. Using your hands, or a rolling pin, knead the dough until it has a consistent texture and roll it out onto a flat barley floured surface until dough is 1/4 inch thick. Using a cookie cutter or using your hands, create small cookies and place them on a greased or parchment lined cookie sheet.

Bake time for these cookies depends upon how thick you make them but averages around 25 minutes.

GROOVY BABY DOG TREATS

1/4 cup of organic Cream of Wheat

3 jars of organic baby food (meat or vegetable, or a mixture.)

Organic chicken or beef

Preheat the oven to 350 degrees.

Add all of the ingredients into a bowl and mix thoroughly. The dough will be thick and pliable, break off small pieces and roll them in to small balls. Place these dough balls on a greased or parchment lined cookie sheet and use a fork to flatten each dough ball just a little (like you would peanut butter cookies).

Bake these treats for 15 minutes or until lightly browned. Cool these treats as you would with human cookies. Then keep them in the refrigerator to keep the ingredients fresh. If you make large batches of these treats they can also be stored in the freezer until ready to use.

***Make sure that baby food doesn't contain garlic, onion, or other ingredients which may be harmful to your dog.

CHICKA CINNA-MINI

1 cup organic almond or oat flour

1 cup low sodium or homemade organic chicken broth

3/4 cup organic oatmeal

1/4 cup organic corn starch

1/4 cup cooking oil or organic olive oil

1 tablespoon baking powder

2 tablespoons organic cinnamon

Preheat oven to 350 degrees.

Add all of the ingredients in to a bowl and mix thoroughly. Flatten out the dough and use cookie cutters to cut out your cookies or break off small pieces of dough and roll them in to cookie shapes. Place the treats on a greased baking tray.

Bake at 350 degrees for 20 minutes.

Allow to cool completely. Store in an airtight container in the refrigerator.

CHICKEN MINIS

3 tablespoons olive oil or coconut oil

1 lb chicken giblets

1/2 cup broth left over from boiling the chicken giblets

1 cup organic whole wheat flour or almond flour

3 organic eggs beaten

1 cup organic flour

1 cup organic cornmeal

Preheat your oven to 450 degrees.

Bring one quart of water to a boil on the stove top and add the chicken giblets. Cook thoroughly and drain, reserving a 1/2 cup of the broth water.

Add the cooked giblets to a blender along with the reserved stock, eggs and olive oil. Blend until you reach a slightly lumpy consistency and then pour in to a large bowl. Add the remaining ingredients into the bowl and mix thoroughly until you get a thicker dough-like mixture. Grease a baking sheet and add smaller spoonfuls of the mixture onto the sheet.

Bake for 20 minutes. These cookies can be stored for up to three days in the refrigerator and freeze the remaining cookies, removing them as needed to defrost in the refrigerator.

HONEY BEE PB COOKIES

1/8 cup water

3 tablespoons unsweetened organic apple sauce

1 large organic egg

1-1/2 cups organic brown rice flour

2 cups organic rolled oats

1 cup natural organic peanut butter

1/4 cup honey or molasses

Preheat your oven to 350 degrees.

While the oven is preheating, add all of the ingredients into a large mixing bowl. Combine the ingredients thoroughly until it achieves a smooth and thick texture. Break off small pieces of the dough and roll them in to small balls. Place the small dough balls on to a greased baking sheet and flatten slightly using your fingers.

Bake for 15 minutes or until light brown. Allow these to cool on a cookie rack and once cool place in an airtight container. These cookies can be frozen to maintain freshness.

SUNFLOWER CUTIES

2 cups organic flour

1/4 cup organic carrots

1 cup organic peanut butter

1 cup organic molasses

1/4 cup organic pumpkin or sunflower seeds

1/2 cup organic apples, chopped

1/4 cup oats ground to a powdered consistency

1 cup organic rolled oats

Preheat oven to 325 degrees.

Add the ingredients listed in a large bowl but leave out the molasses until you have thoroughly mixed dough. Once everything is mixed well, add the molasses and mix it in until the dough has a stiffer consistency. Flour a hard surface and roll out the dough to a 1/4 inch thickness. Use a cookie cutter to cut small cookies or a small knife and place the dough on a greased cookie sheet.

Bake for 30 to 45 minutes. It is also possible to harden these treats using a dehydrator on the highest setting for approximately four hours.

CARROT DOG TREAT MUFFINS

2 cups shredded organic carrots

1/4 cup water

1/4 cup organic dry oats

1 cored and shredded organic apple (remove all seeds)

1/4 cup and 2 tablespoons organic molasses

3/4 cup organic oat or almond flour

1 cup organic flax seed

Preheat oven to 400 degrees.

Add all of the listed ingredients in to a large bowl and mix
thoroughly to create a thick batter. If you have a thinner
batter than you desire, add more almond flour in to the
mix until you achieve a thicker consistency. Add the
mixture in to muffin papers, or to a greased muffin tin,
filling them 3/4 of the way full.

Bake for 15 minutes until brown. Cool, then remove.

APPLE DUMPLIN PRETZELS

The recipe may look like it has a lot of steps, but this 3-ingredient baked treat is easy to make. You can even make your own crazy shapes. Your dog won't care how you twist them — he'll love the taste.

3 cups organic almond flour

1 organic egg

1 cup plain, unsweetened organic applesauce

Preheat oven to 350 degrees.

Line a baking sheet with parchment paper and set aside. Beat egg and set aside. Mix applesauce and almond flour in a large bowl. Pour 1 tablespoon of the egg into a bowl and set aside. Pour the rest of the egg into the bowl with mixed ingredients. Stir the mixture until a dough forms. Take a two-tablespoon-size piece of dough and roll into a tube. Take each tube and make into a "U" shape, then twist the ends together and fold back to the top to make a pretzel shape. Place the pretzels onto the baking tray. Brush the top of each pretzel with the remaining egg.

Bake for approximately 25-30 minutes, until they're slightly browned and firm. Remove from the oven and allow to cool before serving.

CHICKEN LOVER LIVER TREATS

1 organic egg

1 cup organic corn meal

1 cup organic oat or almond flour

1 pound organic chicken livers (If your dog has chicken allergies you can substitute other liver sources such as beef.)

Preheat the oven to 400 degrees.

Begin with liquefying the livers of your choice in a blender or food processor. Next, add the egg and mix well. Add these blended ingredients into a bowl and add the corn meal or corn-meal substitute and flour. Mix well. Grease a deep cookie sheet or jelly-roll pan and pour the mixture in to the pan.

Bake for 15 minutes. Remove the baked treats from the oven and, while they are still warm, cut them in to small squares. This recipe makes a lot of treats so it is important to keep them in an airtight container to keep them fresh. You could also keep any excess treats in a sealed freezer bag in the freezer.

***Tip:* You could always roll this into a dough and cut out shapes prior to baking.*

BLACKBERRY BISCUITS

4 cups organic almond or oat flour

3/4 cup organic flax meal

1/2 cup organic blackberries or blueberries

1/4 cup organic extra virgin olive oil or coconut oil

1 organic egg

Preheat oven to 350 degrees.

Line a baking sheet with parchment paper. Mix all ingredients together with 1 cup water to form a dough. Roll dough until 1/4 inch thick. Cut out biscuits with small cookie cutter. Re-roll remaining dough and cut out more biscuits. Place biscuits 1 inch apart on prepared baking sheet.

Bake for 30 minutes, until nicely browned and firm Remove biscuits from oven and allow to cool before serving.

CRUNCHY APPLE PUPCAKES

2-3/4 cups water

1/4 cup organic applesauce (unsweetened)

2 tablespoons honey

1/8 tablespoon organic vanilla extract

1 medium organic egg

4 cups organic whole wheat or almond flour

1 cup dried organic apple chips (unsweetened)

1 tablespoon organic baking powder

Preheat oven to 350 degrees.

Mix water, applesauce, honey, egg, and vanilla together in a bowl. Add remaining ingredients and mix until well blended. Pour into lightly greased muffin pans.

Bake 1 hour 25 minutes.

FALL PUMPKIN BALLS

1/2 cup canned organic pumpkin

4 tablespoons organic molasses

4 tablespoons water

2 tablespoons organic vegetable oil

2 cups organic whole wheat or almond flour

1/4 teaspoon organic baking soda

1/4 teaspoon organic baking powder

1 teaspoon organic cinnamon (optional)

Preheat oven to 350 degrees.

Mix pumpkin, molasses, vegetable oil, and water together in a bowl. Add the whole wheat flour, baking soda, baking powder and cinnamon to the mixture and stir until dough softens. Scoop out small spoonfuls of dough and roll into balls on your hands (wet hands work best). Set the balls onto a lightly greased cookie sheet and flatten with a fork.

Bake approximately 25 minutes until dough is hardened.

PERKY TURKEY MEAT LOAF

1 lb. ground organic turkey

1 cup cooked organic brown rice

1/4 cup organic carrot, grated

1 teaspoon dried organic basil leaves

1 teaspoon dried organic oregano

1/8 cup dried organic parsley

1/2 cup organic tomato sauce, no salt added

Preheat oven to 350 Degrees.

Mix all ingredients together in a medium bowl. You may want to use your hands to thoroughly combine the ingredients. Spoon the mixture into a 8" x 4" loaf pan. Lightly press mixture into the pan.

Bake for 50 minutes.

Let cool on a wire rack completely before cutting or serving. As with most dog treat recipes with meat, you will need to keep them refrigerated. About 1 week in the refrigerator and 3 months in the freezer will keep them fresher longer.

GROOVY BREATH DOGGY TREATS

2-1/2 cups organic old-fashioned oats

1/2 cup organic fresh parsley, finely chopped

1/2 cup organic fresh mint, finely chopped

1 large organic egg

1/4 cup of water, plus 1 teaspoon

3 tablespoons organic coconut oil

Preheat the oven to 325 Degrees.

Add oats to a blender and pulse to a flour like consistency. In a large bowl whisk together diced parsley and mint, egg, water, and oil. Add oat flour and stir to combine. Knead dough a few times then turn out onto a lightly floured surface.

Using your hands or a rolling pin, flatten dough to about 1/8 inch thick. Using a cookie cutter or knife cut out approximately 40 1-inch mints. Place mints about 1/4 inch apart on a parchment lined or non-stick cookie sheet.

Bake 35-40 minutes, or until golden and crispy.

PRETTY COAT TREATS

1/2 cup organic chicken or beef broth

1/2 cup fat or oil of choice (bacon fat, coconut oil, olive oil, etc.)

1-1/3 cup organic tapioca flour

1/3 cup organic coconut flour

1/2 teaspoon sea salt

2 tablespoons brewers or nutritional yeast

2 tablespoons organic flaxseed meal (sometimes called ground flax or milled flax)

Preheat oven to 400 degrees.

In a small pot over medium heat, bring the chicken broth and fat/oil to a boil. While that is coming to a boil, mix tapioca flour, coconut flour, sea salt, brewer's yeast and flax meal in a medium bowl. Once the broth/fat mixture comes to a boil, remove from heat and add to the flour bowl. Mix well. On a piece of parchment paper, press out the dough into a 1/4 inch thick rectangle. Either cut into squares with a pizza cutter or use cookie cutters in desired shape.

Bake for 15 minutes on a parchment lined cookie sheet. When the timer goes off, shut off the oven, crack the door and leave in the oven until cool (about 10-15 more minutes).

SUGAR'S CHRISTMAS COOKIES

1 cup organic rye flour (substitute rice flour or almond flour)

3/4 teaspoon organic baking powder

1/4 cup organic unsweetened applesauce

2 tablespoons organic honey

3-1/2 tablespoons organic olive oil (or substitute organic canola oil)

2 tablespoons organic dried cranberries, finely chopped

2 tablespoons organic pumpkin seeds

Preheat oven to 350 degrees.

Add the flour, baking powder, applesauce, honey, and olive oil to a mixing bowl. Stir until well combined. Knead dough on a lightly floured surface and roll out to about half an inch thick. Cut treats with a cookie cutter and place on a parchment-lined baking sheet. Firmly press a few pieces of chopped cranberries and pumpkin seeds into the top of each cookie.

Bake for about 12-15 minutes, or until treats are firm to the touch. Turn off oven and open oven door. Allow cookies to cool in oven, about 20-30 minutes. Storage: cookies will keep for several days when stored in a covered airtight container in a cool, dry, shaded location. Cookies may also be frozen: separate treats with parchment paper and store in an airtight covered container.

PEANUT BUTTER SANDWICHES

1-1/4 cup organic almond flour, plus a little extra for cutting dough

1/2 teaspoon organic baking powder

1/2 cup creamy organic peanut butter

1 large organic egg

2 tablespoons honey

1/2 cup organic milk or almond milk

Additional peanut butter for sandwiching

Preheat oven to 350 Degrees.

Line two baking sheets with parchment paper, set aside. In a large bowl (or stand mixer), combine all ingredients, beating until a soft dough forms. Dust counter with flour. Pat out dough into a large rectangle, about 1 inch in depth. Using a 1-1/2 inch circle shaped cookie cutter, cut into circles. Use all dough.

Bake for 10 to 12 minutes, or until they are a uniform color on top (as they bake, the color will actually lighten instead of darken). Transfer to a wire rack and let cool completely.

When your pup deserves a treat, smear a little peanut butter in the center of two cookies and sandwich them together! Store cookies separate from peanut butter for up to two weeks.

EASY PEASY DOGGY TREATS

1-1/2 cups organic oatmeal

2 - 4oz jars organic turkey/chicken & sweet
   potato/pumpkin   baby food

Preheat oven to 350 Degrees.

Grind up the oatmeal in a food processor. Add the
baby food to the food processor and combine with
the oatmeal to create a thick mixture. Use a spoon to
drop balls of the oatmeal mixture onto a baking
sheet.

Bake for approximately 20-22 minutes. Smaller sized
treats will require less time. Cool completely and
store in refrigerator.

****make sure that baby food doesn't contain garlic, onion, or
other ingredients which may be harmful to your dog.*

CAROB PUPCAKES

Pupcake:

2 tablespoons organic carob powder

1/2 cup organic rice flour (organic brown rice or almond
     flour)

1 teaspoon organic baking powder

1/3 cup unrefined organic coconut oil

1/3 cup plain organic Greek yogurt

1 free range or organic egg

Frosting:

3 tablespoons plain organic Greek yogurt

1-1/2 tablespoons creamy organic peanut butter
     (unsalted with no added sugars)

Preheat oven to 350 Degrees
In a small bowl, stir together carob powder, rice flour and
baking powder. In a separate bowl, mix coconut oil,
Greek yogurt and 1 egg until well combined. Add
carob/rice flour mixture and stir until mixed. Spoon
mixture into mini muffin pan.

Bake for 12 minutes.
While pupcakes are baking, prepare frosting by stirring
together Greek yogurt and peanut butter in a small dish.
Transfer frosting to a plastic zip bag, cut a small hole in
one corner and pipe on top of cooled pupcakes.

*** Keep refrigerated in an airtight container for up to 3 days.

 * Note, the coconut oil may begin to surface during baking. If
desired, place pupcakes on a paper towel after baking to absorb.

PB COCO OIL TREATS

1 cup organic coconut oil

1 cup organic all natural peanut butter (unsalted, no sugar).

1 teaspoon ground cinnamon

Add all ingredients to a bowl (double boiler) over pot on stove. Stir until melted and combined.

 Using a tablespoon, pour mixture into silicone baking trays and place in freezer until set.

Store treats in refrigerator.

FRUIT AND VEGGIE TREATS

3/4 cup coconut flour organic

1 teaspoon organic Canola Oil

3/4 cup water

2 organic eggs

1/2 cup organic baby carrots

1-1/2 cups organic spinach

1 organic apple

Preheat your oven to 350 Degrees.

Combine coconut flour, canola oil, eggs and water together in a bowl and mix until your dough is smooth, set aside. Puree or blend together your spinach, apple and carrots.

If you have to add water make sure to drain all the excess water out from your puree mixture. Mix the pureed apple, spinach and carrots together with the dough until evenly combined.

Take a cookie sheet pan and arrange your treats on the sheet using a cookie cutter; or take small pieces of the mixture, roll in your hand, and lie flat to make small round treats.

Bake for about 20-30 minutes until slightly browned and cooked Let cool and feed to your pups!

FRUITY FROZEN TREATS

1/4 cup homemade unsalted chicken broth

1/4 cup water

1/4 cup blueberries

1/2 gala apple

In a small bowl or glass measuring cup, mix together your unsalted chicken stock and water. Wash your fruits and slice your apple into small pieces. Add a couple apple pieces and a couple blueberries to your silicone dog bone molds.

Fill your silicone dog bone molds up with your chicken broth/water mix.

Freeze for about 3 hours. Push up on the bottom of the mold to get your frozen treats out. Let the pups enjoy!

Want to use Homemade Chicken Broth? Here's how:

Don't throw those chicken bones out from dinner! Place your leftover cooked chicken carcass in a large pot and cover with water. Let it simmer for about 90 minutes. Now strain out your broth, discarding all bones and meat. Let your broth cool and there you are!

PEANUT BUTTER POPSICLES

1 cup plain organic yogurt

1 organic banana (chopped into pieces)

1 tablespoon organic peanut butter

Put all ingredients into food processor or blender and mix until well-combined and smooth. Divide the mixture into four paper cups. Position a rawhide stick into the middle of the cup.

Place the cups in the freezer for at least 4 hours.

Peel the paper cup away from the pop and let your pup enjoy.

My Recipe Notes

Perfect Substitutions

_____

_____

_____

_____

_____

_____

_____

_____

_____

_____

_____

_____

_____

_____

_____

_____

_____

_____

_____

ABOUT THE AUTHOR

Joel and Andrea Higginbotham, also known as the Happybothams, live and work in Birmingham, Alabama. We love to laugh and have fun and enjoy every day. Our motto is "Always choose to be happy" because it truly is a choice.

Made in the USA
San Bernardino, CA
19 April 2020